Enclosure

Military Airlift: DOD Plans to Participate in Multi-National Program to Exchange Air Services with European Nations

Information Used in

Briefing to Congressional Committees

September, 2013

GAO
U.S. GOVERNMENT ACCOUNTABILITY OFFICE

441 G St. N.W.
Washington, DC 20548

October 30, 2013

Congressional Committees

Military Airlift: DOD Plans to Participate in Multi-National Program to Exchange Air Services with European Nations

This report formally transmits the enclosed briefing in response to section 1276 of the National Defense Authorization Act for Fiscal Year 2013, which mandates that we conduct a review of the Air Transport, Air-to-Air Refueling and Other Exchange of Services (ATARES) program.[1] ATARES is a European program through which member nations use a system of credits and debits[2] to facilitate sharing of air force-related services—such as troop and cargo airlift—without monetary transactions. ATARES is managed by the Movement Coordination Centre Europe (MCCE), a multi-national organization established in July 2007 to coordinate and optimize the use of airlift, sealift, and land movement assets owned or leased by member nations' militaries. The Department of Defense (DOD) is not a member of ATARES but is seeking to join the program. DOD is a member of MCCE and pays a fee for this membership; there is no additional fee to become a member of ATARES. Currently, because DOD is not a member of ATARES, it utilizes Acquisition and Cross-Servicing Agreements to exchange services with other nations—including ATARES member nations—often through monetary transactions.[3] DOD believes it would benefit from membership in ATARES and requested approval from Congress in 2011 to participate in the program.

Our objectives were to determine (1) the types of services exchanged through ATARES, (2) the extent to which information is available to determine whether ATARES is achieving its intended purposes, and (3) the extent to which information is available on the cost-effectiveness of ATARES. Enclosure 1 details the results of our review based on our briefing to your offices on September 10, 2013.

To address our objectives, we visited U.S. European Command (EUCOM) in Stuttgart, Germany, and MCCE headquarters in Eindhoven, The Netherlands, to interview officials knowledgeable about the ATARES program and to gather documentation and information about the program's operations. EUCOM officials provided us with documentation on how they are currently exchanging air force-related services, including information on EUCOM's participation in Acquisition and Cross-Servicing Agreements. MCCE provided relevant ATARES-related documents, including the Technical Arrangement and Technical Arrangement Annexes, which are the primary documents used to manage the ATARES program. We also reviewed information about ATARES provided by MCCE, such as briefing slides, joining documentation,

---

[1] *See* Pub. L. No. 112-239, § 1276(f) (2013).

[2] A member nation receives credits for services provided to another nation and accrues debits for services provided to it by another member nation.

[3] Acquisition and Cross-Servicing Agreements are international agreements used by DOD to acquire and/or provide logistic support, supplies, and services to/from eligible countries and international organizations.

and meeting minutes. In order to assess the extent to which information was available to determine whether ATARES is achieving its intended purposes and to assess the extent to which information was available on the cost-effectiveness of ATARES, we submitted a set of questions to officials at MCCE and to all 20 ATARES member nations and received written responses from MCCE, Denmark, Italy, Luxembourg, Poland, Sweden, and the United Kingdom. We also interviewed knowledgeable officials from U.S. Transportation Command, U.S. Africa Command, the Office of the Under Secretary of Defense for Policy, the Joint Staff, and the Department of State to obtain their perspectives on ATARES.

We conducted this performance audit from March 2013 to October 2013 in accordance with generally accepted government auditing standards. Those standards require that we plan and perform the audit to obtain sufficient, appropriate evidence to provide a reasonable basis for our findings and conclusions based on our audit objectives. We believe that the evidence obtained provides a reasonable basis for our findings and conclusions based on our audit objectives.

In summary, several air force-related services are exchanged through ATARES, including air transport, air-to-air refueling, maritime patrol, search and air rescue, and strategic air medical evacuation. Since 2001, air transport and air-to-air refueling have comprised more than 80 percent of the services exchanged within the program. ATARES services are exchanged when a request made by one member nation is accepted and executed by another. Member nations report their transactions to MCCE, and MCCE uses this information to track services exchanged through ATARES.

Neither MCCE nor any of the ATARES member nations we met with or received written responses from has conducted comprehensive analyses to assess whether the ATARES program as a whole is achieving its intended purposes. However, some program- and mission-level data on ATARES is collected and tracked, and member nations identified several benefits from the program.[4] MCCE uses the data member nations report about their exchanges of services to ensure that members are operating according to the parameters set by the Technical Arrangement and Annexes to which each member agrees before joining the program. For example, MCCE monitors each nation's balance of credits and debits to ensure that it is not exceeding the 500-hour debit limit on equivalent flying hours set in the annexes to the ATARES Technical Arrangement. MCCE also collects data pertaining to the number of requests and data about mission details, such as the type of asset being used and type of cargo being transported. In addition, MCCE officials stated that member nations appear to benefit from access to additional flight routes, assets, and services. Our audit work identified several benefits that the member nations have attained through participation in ATARES, including saving time and money by efficiently using aircraft assets and increasing cooperation among nations. Although DOD has not yet begun to participate in ATARES, DOD officials stated that the department has several of its own intended purposes for participating in the program, including leveraging empty space on its flights and enhancing multi-national relationships within the European Command area of responsibility.

Neither ATARES officials nor member nations we met with or received written responses from had performed comprehensive analyses to assess the overall cost-effectiveness of the program, but some data on cost savings were available. MCCE reported some cost savings identified by member nations. For example, the United Kingdom and Sweden reported savings, estimating that they each had saved $1.5 million by using the program. Additionally, Belgium and Turkey

---

[4]GAO did not assess the reliability of the data because they did not materially affect the findings, conclusions, or recommendations of this report.

reported that they had saved $71,000 and $256,000, respectively, on specific missions by exchanging services through ATARES. These estimates were provided to us by officials in other countries, and we were not given the data or calculations that had been used to produce them. As a result, we did not assess the reliability of the data used or the credibility of these savings estimates. For additional information on the results of our work, see enclosure I, slide 11.

We requested comments from DOD and MCCE, but none were provided. DOD and MCCE provided technical comments that we incorporated into this report where applicable.

* * * *

We are sending copies of this report to the appropriate congressional committees. We are also sending copies to the Commanders of EUCOM, U.S. Transportation Command, and U.S. Africa Command; the Under Secretary of Defense for Policy; the Chairman, Joint Chiefs of Staff; and the Secretary of State. This report also is available at no charge on the GAO Web site at http://www.gao.gov.

Should you or your staff have any questions concerning this report, please contact me at (202) 512-5431 or russellc@gao.gov. Contact points for our Offices of Congressional Relations and Public Affairs may be found on the last page of this report. Key contributors to this report were Kimberly Seay, Assistant Director; Edward Anderson; Joanne Landesman; Lisa McMillen; Carol Petersen; Michael Shaughnessy; Mike Silver; Yong Song; and Amie Steele.

Cary Russell
Director, Defense Capabilities and Management

Enclosure

List of Committees

The Honorable Carl Levin
Chairman
The Honorable James Inhofe
Ranking Member
Committee on Armed Services
United States Senate

The Honorable Dick Durbin
Chairman
The Honorable Thad Cochran
Ranking Member
Subcommittee on Defense
Committee on Appropriations
United States Senate

The Honorable Howard P. "Buck" McKeon
Chairman
The Honorable Adam Smith
Ranking Member
Committee on Armed Services
House of Representatives

The Honorable Chairman
The Honorable Pete Visclosky
Ranking Member
Subcommittee on Defense
Committee on Appropriations
House of Representatives

Military Airlift: DOD Plans to Participate in Multi-National Program to Exchange Air Services with European Nations

Information Used in

Briefing to Congressional Committees

September, 2013

The Air Transport, Air-to-Air Refueling, and Other Exchange of Services (ATARES) program allows member nations to share air force-related services through a mechanism that facilitates exchange of services without monetary transactions.

- ATARES is managed by the Movement Coordination Centre Europe (MCCE), a multi-national organization established in July 2007 to coordinate and optimize the use of airlift, sealift, and land movement assets owned or leased by member nations' militaries.

- ATARES utilizes a system of credits and debits based on hours flown as the form of exchange among member nations.[1]

- DOD is not a member of the ATARES program but is a member of MCCE.

- DOD is planning to join ATARES, pending approval from the Secretary of Defense and the Secretary of State, per section 1276 of the National Defense Authorization Act for Fiscal Year 2013.[2] DOD officials stated that they did not know when the final approval would occur. In addition to receiving this approval, DOD is to develop the necessary joining documentation and sign the agreements needed to become a member of ATARES.

---

[1] A member nation receives credits for services it provides to another nation and accrues debits for services provided to it by another member nation.
[2] See Pub. L. No. 112-239 (2013). Under section 1276, the Secretary of Defense, with the concurrence of the Secretary of State, may authorize U.S. participation in the ATARES program. See § 1276(a)(1). DOD's participation is limited to reciprocal exchange or transfer of air transportation and air refueling services. See § 1276(a)(2).

2

GAO

Section 1276 of the National Defense Authorization Act for Fiscal Year 2013 mandates that we submit a report on the ATARES program to the congressional defense committees.[3]

In order to address the requirements of the Act, our engagement objectives are:

1. What types of services are exchanged through the ATARES program?

2. To what extent is information available to determine whether ATARES is achieving its intended purposes?

3. To what extent is information available on the cost-effectiveness of the ATARES program?

---

[3]See Pub. L. No. 112-239, § 1276(f).

3

To identify the types of services exchanged through the ATARES program and assess whether information is available to determine whether ATARES is achieving its intended purposes and is cost-effective, we

- reviewed relevant ATARES-related documents, including the ATARES Technical Arrangement, annexes, appendices, briefing slides, joining documentation, meeting minutes, DOD's ATARES Budgetary Impact and Resources paper, and other relevant DOD documents, including Acquisition and Cross-Servicing Agreement guidance, to gather documentation and information about the types of services exchanged through ATARES.

- reviewed written responses to questions we provided to officials at MCCE and to officials at all 20 ATARES member nations. We received responses from MCCE, Denmark, Italy, Luxembourg, Poland, Sweden, and the United Kingdom.

- interviewed knowledgeable officials from MCCE, U.S. European Command (EUCOM), U.S. Transportation Command, U.S. Africa Command, the Office of the Under Secretary of Defense for Policy, the Joint Staff, and the Department of State to obtain their perspectives on the ATARES program.

4

The purpose of the ATARES program, as expressed in the Technical Arrangement, is "to provide a multi-national framework to facilitate mutual support through the exchange of services, in the realm of air force activity, through mutually acceptable arrangements."

- ATARES Technical Arrangement

  - is the overarching document that establishes ATARES and explains the understandings that have been reached among the member nations concerning its administration.

  - replaced an earlier technical arrangement for ATARES signed in 2001 by seven nations: Belgium, France, Germany, Italy, Spain, The Netherlands, and the United Kingdom.

  - has added 13 additional participants since 2001: Austria, the Czech Republic, Denmark, Estonia, Finland, Hungary, Norway, Poland, Slovenia, Sweden, Turkey, Latvia, and Luxembourg (see figure 1).

5

Figure 1: List of Air Transport, Air-to-Air Refueling, and Other Exchange of Services Member Nations

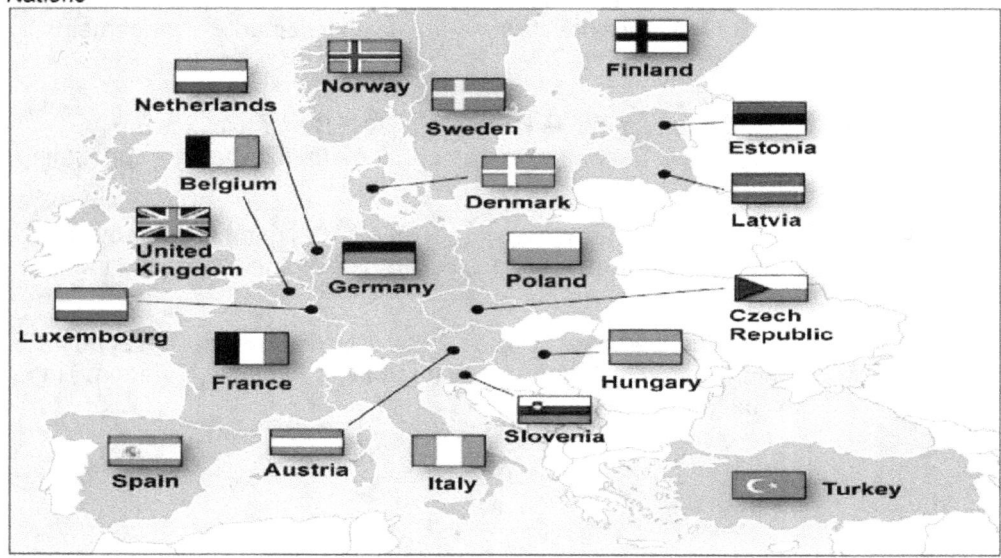

Source: GAO analysis of Movement Coordination Centre Europe data.

6

- Annexes to ATARES Technical Arrangement

  - contain information regarding the agreed-upon administration and coordination of ATARES principles and procedures.

  - include individual nations' procedures for the provision of air transport, air-to-air refueling, and other services.

7

According to DOD officials, EUCOM is working in conjunction with the Joint Staff and the Office of the Secretary of Defense to coordinate DOD's planned participation in the ATARES program. EUCOM will be working with MCCE to develop and gain approval for the joining letter and DOD's appendices to the ATARES technical arrangement annexes.

Section 1276 of the National Defense Authorization Act for Fiscal Year 2013 imposes a limitation on the balance of executed flight hours, whether credits or debits, that DOD may accrue under the program to no more than 500 hours, with the balance for air-to-air refueling not to exceed 200 hours.[4]

However, EUCOM officials stated that in order to mitigate risk, they plan to operate more stringently than the legislation allows.

According to DOD officials, DOD plans to initially participate in the ATARES program with C130 cargo aircraft that are assigned to EUCOM and based in Europe.[5] Other strategic assets, such as those managed by the U.S. Transportation Command, would not be used for ATARES missions.

---

[4]See § 1276(a)(3).
[5]The C130 is a four-engine turboprop military transport aircraft capable of using unprepared runways for takeoffs and landings. It was originally designed as a troop, medical evacuation, and cargo transport aircraft.

8

In addition to planning to join ATARES, DOD is currently involved in other efforts to coordinate air support services with ATARES members and other European nations. For example, according to EUCOM officials, DOD currently utilizes

- Acquisition and Cross-Servicing Agreements[6] to establish bilateral arrangements between DOD and individual ATARES member nations in order to exchange services, including airlift. These agreements often use currency in exchange for services.

- Heavy Airlift Wing – the operational arm of the multinational Strategic Airlift Capability established in 2008 and based at Pápa Air Base, Hungary. It operates three Boeing C-17 cargo jets, providing strategic military airlift capability to 12 member nations (Bulgaria, Lithuania, Estonia, Romania, the United States, Sweden, Finland, Norway, Hungary, Poland, Slovenia, and the Netherlands).

---

[6]Acquisition and Cross-Servicing Agreements are international agreements used by DOD to acquire and/or provide logistic support, supplies, and services to/from eligible countries and international organizations.

9

In addition to ATARES, there are other European air support coordination programs DOD does not participate in that offer similar services. Other programs include the following:

- **European Air Transport Command** – a multinational headquarters organization formed in 2010 to improve the effectiveness and efficiency of the participant nations in the area of air transport, air refueling, and aeromedical evacuation and to maximize the capabilities provided by the five member nations: France, Belgium, the Netherlands, Germany, and Luxembourg.

- **Strategic Airlift Interim Solution** – a multinational airlift consortium that charters six Antonov AN-124-100 transport aircraft, which are capable of handling "outsized" (unusually large) cargo. The consortium includes 12 North Atlantic Treaty Organization (NATO) nations (Belgium, the Czech Republic, France, Germany, Greece, Hungary, Luxembourg, Norway, Poland, Slovakia, Slovenia, and the United Kingdom) and two partner nations (Finland and Sweden).

10

- European member nations are exchanging several air force-related services through the ATARES program, including air transport and air-to-air refueling services.

- Some program- and mission-level data on the program are collected and tracked,[7] although neither MCCE nor any of the ATARES member nations we met with or received written responses from has conducted comprehensive analyses to assess whether ATARES as a whole is achieving its intended purposes. However, member nations have identified several benefits they have attained through their participation in ATARES.

- Although services exchanged through the ATARES program generally do not involve currency,[8] some program- and mission-level cost-related data are collected. Neither MCCE nor any of the member nations we met with or received written responses from has conducted comprehensive analyses to assess the overall cost-effectiveness of the program. However, MCCE and several member nations have identified cost savings they have achieved as a result of their participation in the ATARES program.

---

[7]GAO did not assess the reliability of the data because they did not materially affect the findings, conclusions, or recommendations of this report.
[8]Although the general principle of compensation under ATARES is a balance of exchanged services, cash transfer may be necessary when account balances exceed certain debit limits or a 5-year debit time limit.

11

European member nations are currently exchanging several air force-related services through the ATARES program.

- The primary services exchanged are air transport and air-to-air refueling.
    - Air transport is the movement of cargo and/or passengers.
        - Flights may be destined for countries throughout the world, such as Afghanistan and various African nations.
    - Air-to-air refueling is the process of transferring fuel from one aircraft to another during flight.
    - Since 2001, air transport and air-to-air refueling have represented over 80 percent of ATARES exchanges of services.
- Other ATARES services that members may exchange include the following:
    - Maritime patrol aircraft
    - Search and air rescue
    - Strategic air medical evacuation

12

When a member nation requests an airlift support service through ATARES, the request includes the following:

- **Requesting Participant** – the ATARES member that issues a request for the provision of support.

- **Providing Participant** – the ATARES member that is providing the support requested by the requesting participant.

- **ATARES Authorizer** – the point of contact nominated by a member nation to authorize requests for support and/or authorize the provision of requested support on behalf of the member nation.

- **Executing Authority** – those points of contact tasked by the ATARES authorizer to formulate requests, provide requested support, or execute tasks on behalf of the requesting participant.

13

The ATARES program allows member nations to exchange airlift services with each other through a system of credits and debits.

- The unit of exchange is the **C130 equivalent flying hour**.[9] An equivalent flying hour represents one credit or debit for a member nation.

- For nations that are utilizing other airframes or do not have C130s,[10] an **equivalent factor** must be determined.

    - To determine the equivalent factor, the costs of operating other airframes are compared to the cost of operating a C130.

    - For example, for 2013, Germany's AIRBUS A310 airframe's equivalent factor for air transport is 1.90 (every C130 flying hour equals 1.90 German A310 flying hours).

---

[9]A flying hour is based on the assumption that the C130 will be carrying a full load. For partial loads, other factors are considered.
[10]ATARES member nations that do not have C130 assets are Estonia, Finland, Germany, and Hungary.

14

Exchanges of services are tracked by MCCE using databases, including

- **Effective Visible Execution** – used to track all ATARES air transport-related exchanges.

- **European Planning and Coordination System** – used to track all ATARES-related air-to-air refueling exchanges.

- **ATARES New Accounting and Invoicing System** – provides accounting for all ATARES-related exchanges, including air transport and air-to-air refueling transactions. Both the Effective Visible Execution and European Planning and Coordination systems are linked to the ATARES New Accounting and Invoicing System.

15

 **Objective 2: To what extent is information available to determine whether ATARES is achieving its intended purposes?**

MCCE tracks some data on the program to ensure that members are operating according to the parameters set by the Technical Arrangement and Annexes and ATARES member nations collect some mission-level data. Neither MCCE nor any of the member nations we met with or received written responses from has performed comprehensive analyses to assess whether the ATARES program as a whole is achieving its intended purposes.

- The purpose of ATARES—to provide a multi-national framework to facilitate mutual support through the exchange of services in the realm of air force activity through mutually acceptable arrangements—is described in the ATARES Technical Arrangement.

- The preamble to the Technical Arrangement also contains statements regarding the importance of improving interoperability among participants, the desirability of cooperation in the realm of air activity, and greater cooperation and coordination to increase the effectiveness and affordability of mutual defense activity.

- Each member nation must agree to the terms of the Technical Arrangement in order to participate in ATARES.

16

In addition to the program-wide purpose of ATARES, member nations may have individual goals they hope to achieve by participating in the program.

- Some nations describe individual goals they seek to attain in appendices to the Annexes to the ATARES Technical Arrangement. The Annexes are updated regularly and outline nation-specific procedures and administrative processes for the program, as well as agreed upon parameters for provision of services.

- Based on our audit work, examples of nation-specific goals for participation in ATARES include the following:
    - avoiding monetary exchanges for services and the accompanying administrative work
    - increasing the interoperability of missions and cooperation among nations
    - saving time and money by efficiently sharing assets

17

 **Objective 2: To what extent is information available to determine whether ATARES is meeting its intended purposes?**

Available data indicate that nations benefit from participation in ATARES, but data are not comprehensively analyzed to determine whether the program-wide goals for ATARES or the goals set for the individual nations' participation are being met by the program.

- Various data are tracked by MCCE and individual nations to ensure that ATARES members are operating according to the parameters set by the Technical Arrangement and Annexes.

  - For example, balances of credits and debits are tracked and monitored by MCCE and individual nations to ensure that nations are not exceeding the limits set in an Annex to the ATARES Technical Arrangement.

  - Other data collected and tracked by MCCE to monitor program operations and performance include the following:
    - number of requests for services and offers to provide services
    - matches made for requests and provision of services among nations
    - type of mission, i.e., air transport or air-to-air refueling
    - type of cargo load transported—i.e. full or partial—to determine whether nations are making use of available space on aircraft carrying partial loads.

18

While comprehensive analyses are not conducted by MCCE or by the ATARES member nations we met with or received written responses from, ATARES appears to be beneficial to members in several ways.

- Members are able to access several types of assets and services that are available through ATARES, such as medical evacuation.
- Nations can now access previously-unavailable flight routes by taking advantage of available space on the aircraft of other nations that can fly such routes.
- Interoperability among nations that enables them to leverage each others' airlift missions has reportedly increased.
- According to MCCE officials, the diplomatic clearance process for cargo transport has been simplified for some nations.

19

 **GAO**

Although DOD has not yet begun to participate in ATARES, officials stated that the department has several of its own intended purposes for program participation, including

- taking advantage of available space on its own and other nations' aircraft to more efficiently transport supplies and passengers.
- maintaining or enhancing multi-national relationships and cooperation, especially as operations in Afghanistan continue to decrease.
- potentially consolidating multi-national diplomatic clearance processes for the handling and transportation of cargo and passengers to reduce the time and workload spent on meeting different nations' standards.
- potentially expanding access to air services where ATARES member nations currently conduct operations in other theaters, such as U.S. Africa Command.
- potentially reducing the use of existing Acquisition and Cross-Servicing Agreements established with current ATARES member nations.

20

Although neither ATARES officials nor member nations we met with or received written responses from had performed comprehensive analyses to assess the overall cost-effectiveness of the program, some data on cost savings were available.[11]

- MCCE and member nation officials we met with were unaware of any cost-effectiveness assessments of the ATARES program.

- MCCE reported some cost savings identified by member nations.

  - Belgium reported that it saved 55,000 euro (approximately $71,000) utilizing transport exchange service provided by the Heavy Airlift Wing using Dutch flying hours to transport 13 tons of general cargo from Hungary to Afghanistan.

  - Turkey reported that it saved 200,000 euro (approximately $256,000) utilizing transport exchange service provided by a Belgian AN124 to transport 70 tons of cargo from Turkey to Afghanistan.

  - Norwegian officials estimate that Norway saves 3-3.5 million euro (approximately $3.85-$4.49 million) annually through its participation in the ATARES program.

---

[11]These estimates were provided to us by officials in other countries, and we were not given the data or calculations that had been used to produce them. As a result, we did not assess the reliability of the data used or the credibility of these savings estimates.

21

- In responses to the written questions we provided and interviews with officials in ATARES member nations, three member nations reported cost savings.[12]

    - Sweden estimated that it has saved 1.2 million euro (approximately $1.5 million) since joining the ATARES program in 2007.

    - The United Kingdom estimated that it has saved 1 million pounds (approximately $1.5 million) since fiscal year 2009/2010.

    - The Netherlands stated that it saves "millions" of euro annually through its participation in the ATARES program.

---

[12]We sent a set of questions related to the performance of ATARES to officials in all ATARES member nations regarding the program. Six nations provided responses; two of these nations cited cost savings. The savings cited for the Netherlands were reported by a Dutch official during an interview.

22

(351807)

GAO's Mission	The Government Accountability Office, the audit, evaluation, and investigative arm of Congress, exists to support Congress in meeting its constitutional responsibilities and to help improve the performance and accountability of the federal government for the American people. GAO examines the use of public funds; evaluates federal programs and policies; and provides analyses, recommendations, and other assistance to help Congress make informed oversight, policy, and funding decisions. GAO's commitment to good government is reflected in its core values of accountability, integrity, and reliability.
Obtaining Copies of GAO Reports and Testimony	The fastest and easiest way to obtain copies of GAO documents at no cost is through GAO's website (www.gao.gov). Each weekday afternoon, GAO posts on its website newly released reports, testimony, and correspondence. To have GAO e-mail you a list of newly posted products, go to www.gao.gov and select "E-mail Updates."
Order by Phone	The price of each GAO publication reflects GAO's actual cost of production and distribution and depends on the number of pages in the publication and whether the publication is printed in color or black and white. Pricing and ordering information is posted on GAO's website, http://www.gao.gov/ordering.htm.
	Place orders by calling (202) 512-6000, toll free (866) 801-7077, or TDD (202) 512-2537.
	Orders may be paid for using American Express, Discover Card, MasterCard, Visa, check, or money order. Call for additional information.
Connect with GAO	Connect with GAO on Facebook, Flickr, Twitter, and YouTube. Subscribe to our RSS Feeds or E-mail Updates. Listen to our Podcasts. Visit GAO on the web at www.gao.gov.
To Report Fraud, Waste, and Abuse in Federal Programs	Contact: Website: www.gao.gov/fraudnet/fraudnet.htm E-mail: fraudnet@gao.gov Automated answering system: (800) 424-5454 or (202) 512-7470
Congressional Relations	Katherine Siggerud, Managing Director, siggerudk@gao.gov, (202) 512-4400, U.S. Government Accountability Office, 441 G Street NW, Room 7125, Washington, DC 20548
Public Affairs	Chuck Young, Managing Director, youngc1@gao.gov, (202) 512-4800 U.S. Government Accountability Office, 441 G Street NW, Room 7149 Washington, DC 20548